cozy weighted blankets

LEISURE ARTS, INC. • Maumelle, Arkansas

Relax and get cozy with the stress- free snuggle of a weighted blanket!

Transform your relaxation with 15 family friendly projects destined to bring tranquil serenity to your downtime. Even the most restless sleepers deserve stress-free and sleep-filled evenings, so craft your own weighted blanket, and avoid paying the high cost of ready-made blankets! From family sized wraps to throws just for you, you'll find your perfect replacement to that childhood stuffed animal and fill your downtime with calming cuddles instead of restless tosses and turns.

Why a Weighted Blanket?

A weighted blanket molds to your body like a warm hug. Doctors and therapists believe that the pressure helps relax the nervous system and causes the brain to release neurotransmitters like serotonin and dopamine that improve moods and induce a calming effect. This helps many people relax naturally.

Weighted blankets are often used by people with autism, Asperger's syndrome, restless leg syndrome, chronic pain, anxiety, stress, sensory processing disorders, and many other conditions. Many people use them just because they believe the weight of the blanket helps them sleep better.

Consult your doctor or occupational therapist regarding using a weighted blanket - the correct size, the correct weight, and the duration for use. Do not use a weighted blanket if you have respiratory, circulatory, or temperature regulation problems, or post surgery. We do not recommend weighted blankets for children younger than 6 years of age. Never leave a small child unattended when using a weighted blanket. Make sure the child is strong enough to push the blanket off, if necessary.

contents

SUPPLIES

Fabrics

For our blanket tops, we used quilt weight 100% cotton fabrics, beautiful wool flannels, and plush, "sensory" fabrics, such as, fleece, minky, or chenille. Plush fabrics are available in solids, prints, embossed, and double-sided. For the backing, quilt weight 100% cotton fabric or 100% cotton flannel is suitable but a plush fabric is also very desirable.

Plastic Poly Pellets

Use safe, non-toxic hypo-allergenic polypropylene pellets for your weighed blanket.

Digital Food Scale

For accuracy, use a digital food scale to weigh the pellets to put in each pouch.

Sewing Machine Needles

Use a size 10 (70) needle for piecing the blocks. Use a size 14 (90) denim needle for sewing the blanket top and backing together. Denim needles have a sharp point and a strong shaft that can stitch through many layers without breaking. If using a plush fabric, use a 90/14 ballpoint needle. A ballpoint needle has a rounded tip that eliminates damage to the fabric while sewing. Try to avoid hitting the poly pellets as you sew.

Thread

When sewing quilt weight 100% cotton fabrics for the blanket top, use all-purpose sewing thread in both the needle and the bobbin. All-purpose thread is also suitable for sewing the blanket top to a quilt weight 100% cotton backing.

If using a plush fabric, use 100% polyester thread in both the needle and the bobbin.

Walking Foot or Even Feed Foot

Use a walking foot on your machine when sewing the blanket top to the backing. This foot will help eliminate puckering and helps feed the fabric layers together at the same time.

Wrapping Paper Tube

Use a wrapping paper tube to help feed the pellets into the channels of the blanket. A piece of PVC pipe or a vacuum cleaner extension tube can also be used.

Kitchen Funnel

You may find it helpful to tape a kitchen funnel to the end of the wrapping paper tube. This will help reduce spilling.

DETERMINING THE BLANKET SIZE

A weighted blanket can be used by laying it across the lap or torso, wrapping it around the shoulders, covering just the legs, or covering the entire body for sleeping. If using the weighted blanket for sleeping, the blanket should fit the body, not the bed. It should be big enough to cover the body from the tip of the chin to just past the toes. But children grow quickly; you may choose to allow a little extra length for growing room.

Choose the size depending on the intended use and the height of the user.

DETERMINING THE BLANKET WEIGHT

Consult your healthcare professional to determine the best weight blanket to make. For children and young teens, we recommend the pellets in your blanket weigh 10% of the body weight plus 1 pound. For older teens and adults this formula may become very heavy. These blankets should be 5%-10% of your body weight but should not exceed 20 pounds.

Convert the desired weight in pounds to ounces by multiplying the weight by 16 oz. Divide the total ounces by the number of pouches given in the project instructions. Use the food scale to determine the amount of pellets. Place this amount in each pouch.

For example:
A 50 lb. child would require 6 pounds of pellets
(50 lb. x 10% + 1 lb. = 6 lbs.)

Multiply the weight by 16 oz. (6 lb. x 16 oz. = 96 oz.)

Divide the total ounces by the number of pouches stated in the project instructions for the size blanket you are making. (96 oz. ÷ 117 pouches = 0.82 oz. per pouch.) Place the determined number of ounces in each pouch.

TIP: To speed up the process, find a container to scoop and measure the pellets for each pouch. This could be a measuring cup or a foam cup on which you have marked a line.

PREPARING THE FABRICS

We recommend that all fabrics be washed and dried before cutting. If fabrics are not pre-washed, washing the finished blanket may cause shrinkage. Bright and dark colors, which may run, should always be washed before cutting. Cotton fabrics should be washed using warm water and tumble dried on low. Cotton fabrics need to be pressed after washing. Plush fabrics should be washed using cold water and tumble dried on low or hung to dry. Plush fabrics **should not** be pressed as they can melt when exposed to the high heat of the iron. If pressing is necessary, use low temperature and a press cloth. After washing and drying fabric, fold lengthwise with wrong sides together and matching selvages for cutting.

TIPS FOR CUTTING AND SEWING PLUSH FABRICS

Cutting

- When cutting, plush fabrics can create lots of lint. When finished cutting, shake the fabric pieces gently over your cutting area to remove the lint. Use a lint roller to clean up your cutting and sewing surfaces.
- Fleece may have nap. Nap refers to a fabric that has a furry or downy surface. If you brush one way with your hand, the fabric feels smooth and will appear one way. If you brush the opposite way, the fabric is rough and will appear different. If your fleece has nap, all the pieces must be laid in the same direction for cutting and when sewing. Make sure the nap runs the same direction on the front and back of the blanket.

Sewing

Plush fabrics tend to be very stretchy. They often require special handling when sewing to prevent stretching and to keep the top and bottom layers of the fabric feeding evenly through your machine. The following tips will make your sewing easier.

- To determine the right side of fleece, stretch the cut edge of the fabric slightly. Fleece will roll to the wrong side.
- Increase your stitch length. Set stitch length for approximately 8-10 stitches per inch.
- Adjust the tension. To adjust the tension, turn the regulator dial. The lower the number, the looser the tension.
- Lessen the pressure on your presser foot. The presser foot holds the fabric against the feed dogs while sewing. Lessening the pressure will allow the fabric to feed through the machine with less stretching.
- Use a stiletto or the sharp end of your seam ripper to press down on the fabric in front of the presser foot.
- You can use a straight stitch, a stretch stitch, or a narrow zigzag stitch when sewing plush fabric.
- Refer to project instructions for seam allowance width.
- Use long straight pins or Clover® Wonder Clips to pin the raw edges of the blanket together. Pin every 1" to 1½". Place a second row of pins approximately 2" from the raw edges of the blanket. Pin, pin, pin, and pin some more.
- Adjust the speed of your machine. Sew slowly so you can see if your fabric is stretching as you go.
- To press fleece, place the fabric right side down on a plush bath towel and press with iron using low temperature and a press cloth. If the fabric has raised dots, ironing may flatten the dots.

ROTARY CUTTING

While a rotary cutter and ruler can be used to cut the blanket backing, these instructions primarily pertain to cutting the pieces for the blocks.

- Place fabric on work surface with fold closest to you.
- Cut all strips from the selvage-to-selvage width of the fabric unless otherwise indicated in project instructions.
- Square left edge of fabric using rotary cutter and rulers **(Figs. 1-2)**.
- To cut each strip required for a project, place ruler over cut edge of fabric, aligning desired marking on ruler with cut edge; make cut **(Fig. 3)**.
- If cutting several strips from a single piece of fabric, it is important to make sure that cuts remain at a perfect right angle to the fold; square fabric as needed.

Fig. 1

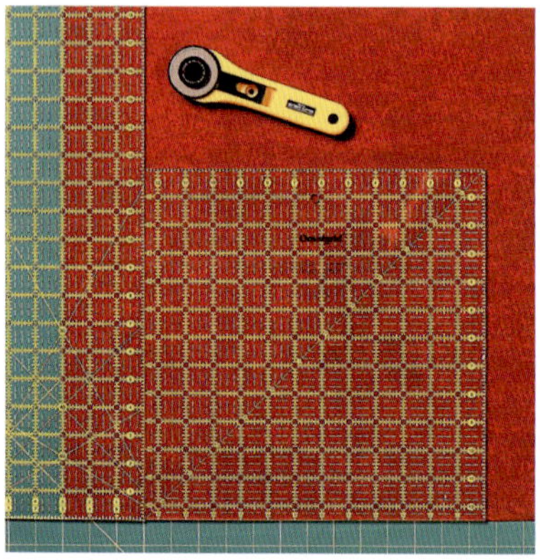

Fig. 2

Fig. 3

PIECING THE BLOCKS

Precise cutting, followed by accurate piecing, will ensure that all pieces of blanket top fit together well.

- Use a size 10 (70) sewing machine needle for piecing the blocks.
- For most sewing, set sewing machine stitch length for approximately 11 stitches per inch.
- Use all-purpose sewing thread (not quilting thread) in needle and in bobbin.
- An accurate $^{1}/_{4}$" seam allowance is essential. Presser feet that are $^{1}/_{4}$" wide are available for most sewing machines.
- When piecing, always place pieces right sides together and match raw edges; pin if necessary.
- Chain piecing saves time and will usually result in more accurate piecing.
- Trim away points of seam allowances that extend beyond edges of sewn pieces.

Sewing Across Seam Intersections

When sewing across intersection of two seams, place pieces right sides together and match seams exactly, making sure seam allowances are pressed in opposite directions **(Fig. 4)**.

Sewing Sharp Points

To ensure sharp points when joining triangular or diagonal pieces, stitch across the center of the "X" (shown in pink) formed on wrong side by previous seams **(Fig. 5)**.

Pressing

- Use steam iron set on "Cotton" when pressing cotton fabrics.
- When piecing the blanket top, press after sewing each seam. Seam allowances are almost always pressed to one side, usually toward the darker fabric. However, to reduce bulk it may occasionally be necessary to press seam allowances toward the lighter fabric or even to press them open. To prevent the dark fabric seam allowance from showing through light fabric, trim darker seam allowance slightly narrower than lighter seam allowance.

Fig. 4

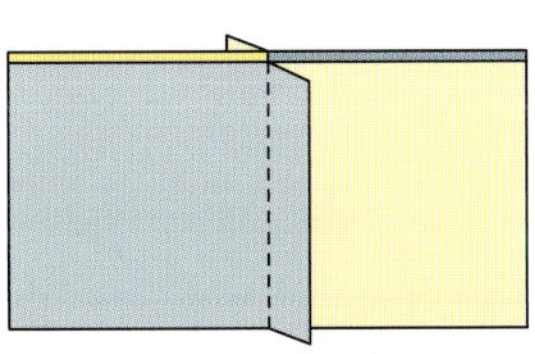

Fig. 5

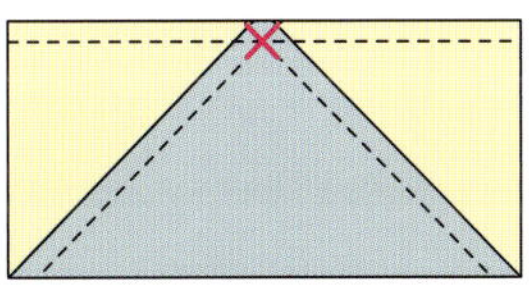

MARKING STITCHING LINES

Stitching lines for vertical and horizontal channels may be marked using fabric marking pencils, chalk markers, or water- or air-soluble pens. Stitching lines may also be marked with $^1/_4$" quilter's tape or painter's tape. Simply lay the tape across the fabric where the stitching line is desired and use the edge of the tape to stitch along.

Caution: Pressing may permanently set some marks. Test different markers on scrap fabric to find one that marks clearly and can be thoroughly removed.

ASSEMBLING THE BLANKET

Attach a walking foot to your sewing machine. Backstitch at beginning and end of stitching. Refer to project instructions for seam allowance width.

1. Follow project instructions to assemble Blanket Top.

2. If the backing for the blanket is 40" wide or more, two lengths will need to be pieced together for the backing. Cut the fabric into two equal lengths. Match right sides and raw edges and sew lengths together. Trim backing to size given in project instructions.

3. Press 1 short edge of Blanket Top and **backing** $^1/_4$" to wrong side, unless otherwise specified.

4. Matching right sides and pressed edges, sew Blanket Top to backing along long edges and unpressed short edge **(Fig. 6)**. Clip corners, turn right side out, and press. *(**Note:** If using a plush fabric backing, sew with the plush fabric on the bottom and the cotton fabrics on the top. Sometimes the plush fabric will stretch or shift. To help prevent this, lengthen your stitch length and pin layers together every 1" to $1^1/_2$". Place a second row of pins approximately 2" from the raw edges of the blanket. It may also be helpful to reduce the presser foot pressure.)*

Fig. 6

5. The project instructions will tell you where to mark the vertical and horizontal channels. The placement of the vertical and horizontal channels will depend on the size of the blanket, the number of blocks, and the number of seams in the blocks. Often the stitching line will be on a seamline; this should be done directly on the seamline or just to the side of the seamline opposite the seam allowances. This stitching line does not have to be marked. Refer to **Fig. 7** and follow the project instructions to mark and stitch the vertical channels.

6. Follow project instructions to mark the horizontal channels on the blanket top.

7. Tape the kitchen funnel to the end of the wrapping paper tube. Place the tube in the first channel on one side. Pour the determined amount of pellets in the tube. Let the pellets fall all the way to the bottom of the channel. Work side to side to fill each channel. Keeping the pellets out of the way, stitch a horizontal channel to form the first row of pouches **(Fig. 8)**.

8. Pour pellets in each vertical channel again. Let them fall all the way to the bottom. Stitch a horizontal channel to form the next row of pouches.

9. Continue filling and sewing horizontal channels until all the pouches are filled **(Fig. 9)**.

10. After filling the final pouches, topstitch the pressed edges closed.

LAUNDERING

Your blanket can be machine washed, separately, in a cool wash with gentle detergent (no chlorine bleach or fabric softener). For large blankets, it may be best to use a commercial size machine. To dry, hang evenly over laundry line. To help maintain shape, do not hang from one edge.

TIP: You may find it helpful to slide a pencil across the fabric and push the pellets to the bottom of the pouches as you sew. You can also insert a row of pins to hold the pellets at the bottom.

Fig. 7

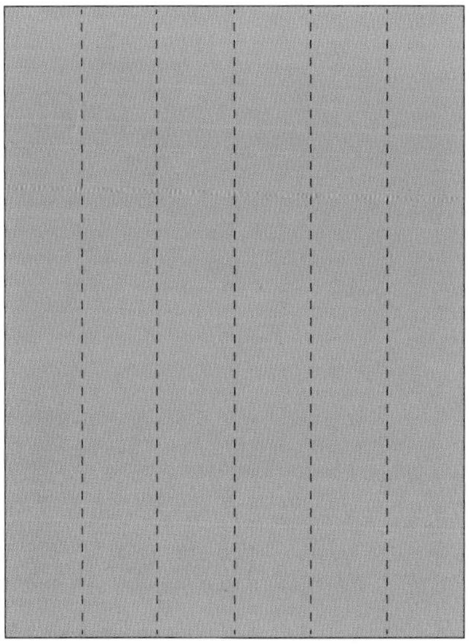

Fig. 8

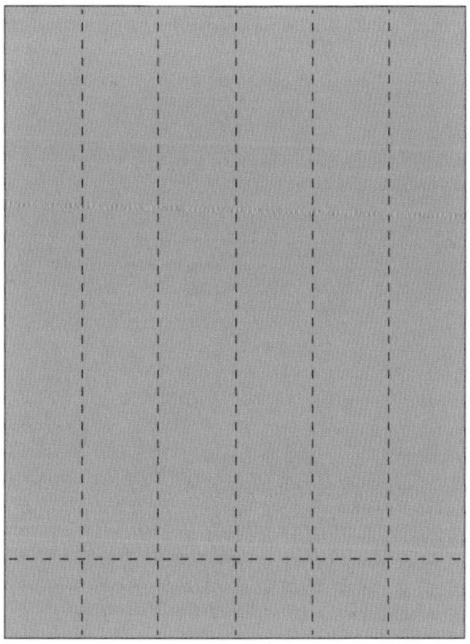

Fig. 9

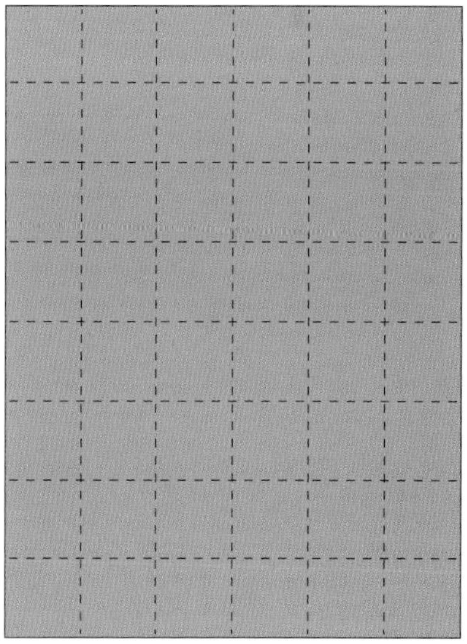

super *simple*

Youth Small, Finished Size: 36" x 48" (91 cm x 122 cm)

For information on other blanket sizes, refer to the table on page 18.

SHOPPING LIST

Yardage is based on 43"/44" (109 cm/112 cm) wide fabric with a usable width of 40" (102 cm).

- ☐ 1 5/8 yds (1.5 m) of fabric for blanket top
- ☐ 1 5/8 yds (1.5 m) of fabric for backing
- ☐ plastic poly pellets (see **Step 1**)
- ☐ walking foot
- ☐ size 14 (90) denim sewing machine needle
- ☐ wrapping paper tube
- ☐ kitchen funnel
- ☐ measuring cup
- ☐ water-soluble fabric marking pen

CUTTING THE PIECES

*Follow **Rotary Cutting**, page 12, to cut fabric. All measurements include 1/2" seam allowances.*

From fabric for blanket top:

- Cut **blanket top** 37" x 49".

From fabric for backing:

- Cut **backing** 37" x 49".

ASSEMBLING THE BLANKET

Read pages 8-15, before beginning your blanket. Use 1/2" seam allowances throughout.

1. Refer to **Determining the Blanket Weight**, page 9, to determine the quantity of pellets needed for the blanket and how much to place in each pouch. This blanket has 108 pouches.

2. *Refer to **Assembling the Blanket**, pages 14-15, to assemble, fill, and close the blanket.* After sewing blanket top to backing, mark the vertical and horizontal stitching lines (shown in red) 4" apart on the blanket top **(Fig. 1)**. Stitch vertically along each marked line to make 9 vertical channels. Place determined amount of pellets in each channel. Stitch horizontally along each marked line to make 12 horizontal channels. Close the blanket.

Fig. 1

The following table provides the information necessary to make your blanket in other sizes.

	Youth Medium	Youth Large	Adult Small	Adult Medium	Adult Large	Adult X-Large
Finished Size	36" x 52"	36" x 56"	40" x 60"	44" x 64"	48" x 68"	52" x 72"
Fabric Requirements	$1^5/_8$ yds (1.5 m) of fabric for blanket top $1^5/_8$ yds (1.5 m) of fabric for backing	$1^3/_4$ yds (1.6 m) of fabric for blanket top $1^3/_4$ yds (1.6 m) of fabric for backing	$1^7/_8$ yds (1.7 m) of fabric for blanket top $1^7/_8$ yds (1.7 m) of fabric for backing	$3^7/_8$ yds (3.5 m) of fabric for blanket top $3^7/_8$ yds (3.5 m) of fabric for backing	$4^1/_8$ yds (3.8 m) of fabric for blanket top $4^1/_8$ yds (3.8 m) of fabric for backing	$4^3/_8$ yds (4 m) of fabric for blanket top $4^3/_8$ yds (4 m) of fabric for backing
Channel Grid	9 x 13	9 x 14	10 x 15	11 x 16	12 x 17	13 x 18
Pellet Pouches	117	126	150	176	204	234
Blanket Top Cut Size	37" x 53"	37" x 57"	41" x 61"	45" x 65", pieced as necessary	49" x 69", pieced as necessary	53" x 73", pieced as necessary
Backing Cut Size	37" x 53"	37" x 57"	41" x 61"	45" x 65", pieced as necessary	49" x 69", pieced as necessary	53" x 73", pieced as necessary

family *Blanket*

Adult Extra-Large, Finished Size: 49" x 77" (124 cm x 196 cm)

SHOPPING LIST

Yardage is based on 58"/60" (147 cm/152 cm) wide fabric with a usable width of 56" (142 cm).

- ☐ 4³/₈ yds (4 m) of gray solid plush fleece for blanket top and backing

You will also need:

- ☐ plastic poly pellets (see **Step 1**)
- ☐ walking foot
- ☐ size 14 (90) ballpoint sewing machine needle
- ☐ wrapping paper tube
- ☐ kitchen funnel
- ☐ measuring cup
- ☐ water-soluble fabric marking pen

CUTTING THE PIECES

*Follow **Rotary Cutting**, page 12, to cut fabric. All measurements include ¹/₂" seam allowances.*

From gray solid plush fabric:

- Cut two pieces 50" x 78" for **blanket top** and **backing**.

ASSEMBLING THE LAP BLANKET TOP

Read pages 8-15 before beginning your blanket. Use ¹/₂" seam allowances throughout.

1. *Refer to **Determining the Blanket Weight**, page 9, to determine the quantity of pellets needed for the blanket and how much to place in each pouch. This blanket has 77 pouches.*

2. *Refer to **Assembling the Blanket**, pages 14-15, to assemble, fill and close the blanket.* After sewing blanket top to backing, mark the vertical and horizontal stitching lines (shown in red) 7" apart on the blanket top **(Fig. 1)**. Stitch vertically along each marked line to make 7 vertical channels. Place determined amount of pellets in each channel. Stitch horizontally along each marked line to make 11 horizontal channels. Close the blanket. Topstitch ¹/₂" from edge of blanket on all sides, if desired.

Fig. 1

teal squares

Youth Medium/Adult Small, Finished Size: 38" x 57" (97 cm x 145 cm)
Finished Block Size: 9$^{1}/_{2}$" x 9$^{1}/_{2}$" (24 cm x 24 cm)
For information on other blanket sizes, refer to the table below.

SHOPPING LIST

Yardage is based on 43"/44" (109 cm/112 cm) wide fabric with a usable width of 40" (102 cm). Layer Cakes are approximately 10" x 10" (25 cm x 25 cm).

- ☐ 1 Layer Cake or $^{5}/_{8}$ yd (57 cm) **each** of four assorted prints
- ☐ 1$^{3}/_{4}$ yds (1.6 m) of fabric for backing
- ☐ plastic poly pellets (see **Step 3**)
- ☐ walking foot
- ☐ size 10 (70) sewing machine needle and size 14 (90) denim sewing machine needle
- ☐ wrapping paper tube
- ☐ kitchen funnel
- ☐ measuring cup
- ☐ water-soluble fabric marking pen

ASSEMBLING THE BLANKET

Read pages 8-15 before beginning your blanket. Use 1/4" seam allowances throughout.

1. Sew 4 **squares** together to make a Row. Make 6 Rows. Press seam allowances in one direction.

2. Alternating direction of seam allowances, sew Rows together to make the **Blanket Top**.

3. Refer to **Determining the Blanket Weight**, page 9, to determine the quantity of pellets needed for the blanket and how much to place in each pouch. This blanket has 96 pouches.

4. *Refer to **Assembling the Blanket**, pages 14-15, to assemble, fill, and close the blanket.* After sewing blanket top to backing, mark the vertical and horizontal stitching lines (shown in red) across each square **(Fig. 1)**. Stitch vertically between each block on the seamline and across the squares vertically where marked to make 8 vertical channels. Place determined amount of pellets in each channel. Stitch horizontally between each block on the seamline and across the squares horizontally where marked to make 12 horizontal channels. Close the blanket.

Blanket Top

Fig. 1

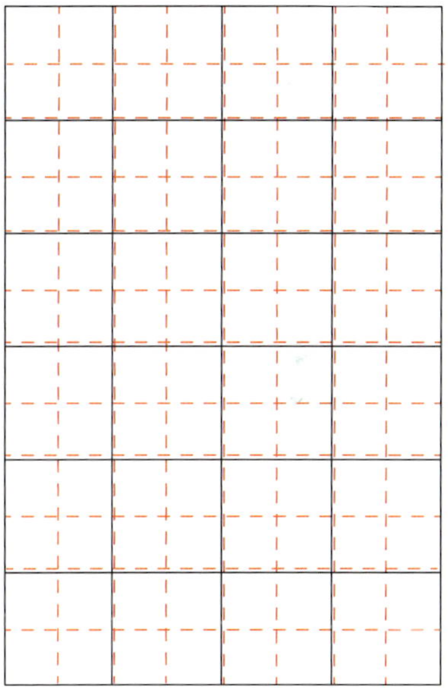

The following table provides the information necessary to make your blanket in other sizes.

	Youth Small	Youth Large	Adult Medium	Adult Large	Adult X-Large
Finished Size	38" x 47$^1/_2$"	38" x 66$^1/_2$"	47$^1/_2$" x 66$^1/_2$"	47$^1/_2$" x 76"	57" x 76"
Fabric Requirements	1 Layer Cake **or** $^5/_8$ yd (57 cm) **each** of four assorted prints 1$^1/_2$ yds (1.4 m) of fabric for backing	1 Layer Cake **or** $^5/_8$ yd (57 cm) **each** of four assorted prints 2 yds (1.8 m) of fabric for backing	1 Layer Cake **or** 1 yd (91 cm) **each** of four assorted prints 4 yds (3.7 m) of fabric for backing	1 Layer Cake **or** 1 yd (91 cm) **each** of four assorted prints 4$^1/_2$ yds (4.1 m) of fabric for backing	2 Layer Cakes **or** 1 yd (91 cm) **each** of four assorted prints 4$^1/_2$ yds (4.1 m) of fabric for backing
Number of Blocks	20	28	35	40	48
Block Set	4 x 5	4 x 7	5 x 7	5 x 8	6 x 8
Pellet Pouches	80	112	140	160	192
Each of Four Assorted Prints	5 **squares** 10" x 10"	7 **squares** 10" x 10"	9 **squares** 10" x 10"; you will use 35	10 **squares** 10" x 10"	12 **squares** 10" x 10"
Backing Cut Size	38$^1/_2$" x 48"	38$^1/_2$" x 67"	48" x 67", pieced as necessary	48" x 76$^1/_2$", pieced as necessary	57$^1/_2$" x 76$^1/_2$", pieced as necessary

charm squares

Youth Small, Finished Size: 36" x 45" (91 cm x 114 cm)
Finished Block Size: $4^1/_2$" x $4^1/_2$" (11 cm x 11 cm)
For information on other blanket sizes, refer to the table below.

SHOPPING LIST

Yardage is based on 43"/44" (109 cm/112 cm) wide fabric with a usable width of 40" (102 cm). Charm squares are approximately 5" x 5" (13 cm x 13 cm).

- ☐ 80 assorted charm squares **or** 5" x 5" (13 cm x 13 cm) squares
- ☐ $1^3/_8$ yds (1.3 m) of fabric for backing
- ☐ plastic poly pellets (see **Step 3**)
- ☐ size 10 (70) sewing machine needle and size 14 (90) denim sewing machine needle
- ☐ walking foot
- ☐ wrapping paper tube
- ☐ kitchen funnel
- ☐ measuring cup

CUTTING THE PIECES

*Follow **Rotary Cutting**, page 12, to cut fabric. All measurements include $^1/_4$" seam allowances.*

From fabric for backing:

- Cut **backing** $36^1/_2$" x $45^1/_2$".

ASSEMBLING THE BLANKET

Read pages 8-15 before beginning your blanket. Use 1/4" seam allowances throughout.

1. Sew 8 squares together to make a **Row**. Make 10 Rows. Press seam allowances in alternating directions.

2. Sew Rows together to make **Blanket Top**. Press all seam allowances toward bottom.

3. Refer to **Determining the Blanket Weight**, page 9, to determine the quantity of pellets needed for the blanket and how much to place in each pouch. This blanket has 80 pouches.

4. *Refer to **Assembling the Blanket**, pages 14-15, to assemble, fill, and close the blanket.* After sewing blanket top to backing, stitch along each vertical seamline (shown in red) to make 8 vertical channels **(Fig. 1)**. Place determined amount of pellets in each channel. Stitch horizontally along each horizontal seamline (shown in red) to make 10 horizontal channels. Close the blanket.

Row

Blanket Top

Fig. 1

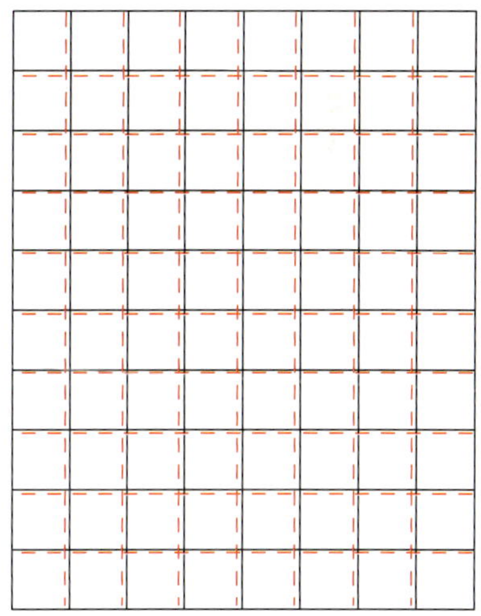

The following table provides the information necessary to make your blanket in other sizes.

	Youth Medium or Adult Small	Youth Large or Adult Medium	Adult Large	Adult X-Large
Finished Size	36" x 54"	36" x 63"	45" x 72"	54" x 72"
Fabric Requirements	3 Charm Packs **or** 96 assorted 5" x 5" (13 cm x 13 cm) squares 1 3/4 yds (1.6 m) of fabric for backing	3 Charm Packs **or** 112 assorted 5" x 5" (13 cm x 13 cm) squares 2 yds (1.8 m) of fabric for backing	4 Charm Packs **or** 160 assorted 5" x 5" (13 cm x 13 cm) squares 4 3/8 yds (4 m) of fabric for backing	5 Charm Packs **or** 192 assorted 5" x 5" (13 cm x 13 cm) squares 4 3/8 yds (4 m) of fabric for backing
Square Set	8 x 12	8 x 14	10 x 16	12 x 16
Pellet Pouches	96	112	160	192
Backing Cut Size	36 1/2" x 54 1/2"	36 1/2" x 63 1/2"	45 1/2" x 72 1/2", pieced as necessary	54 1/2" x 72 1/2", pieced as necessary

plaid flannels

Adult Extra-Large, Finished Size: 50" x 80" (127 cm x 203 cm)
Finished Block Size: 10" x 10" (25 cm x 25 cm)
For information on other blanket sizes, refer to the table on page 29.

SHOPPING LIST

Yardage is based on 43"/44" (109 cm/112 cm) wide fabric with a usable width of 40" (102 cm). Fat quarters are approximately 22" x 18" (56 cm x 46 cm.)

- ☐ 20 fat quarters of assorted light and dark plaid flannel fabrics for blocks
- ☐ 4¾ yds (4.3 m) of fabric for backing
- ☐ plastic poly pellets (see **Step 8**, page 28)
- ☐ walking foot
- ☐ size 10 (70) sewing machine needle and size 14 (90) denim sewing machine needle
- ☐ wrapping paper tube
- ☐ kitchen funnel
- ☐ measuring cup
- ☐ water-soluble fabric marking pen

CUTTING THE PIECES

*Follow **Rotary Cutting**, page 12, to cut fabric. Refer to **Cutting Diagram** to cut each fat quarter.*

From each fat quarter:

- Cut 1 **large square** 10½" x 10½".
- Cut 4 **small squares** 5½" x 5½".

Cutting Diagram

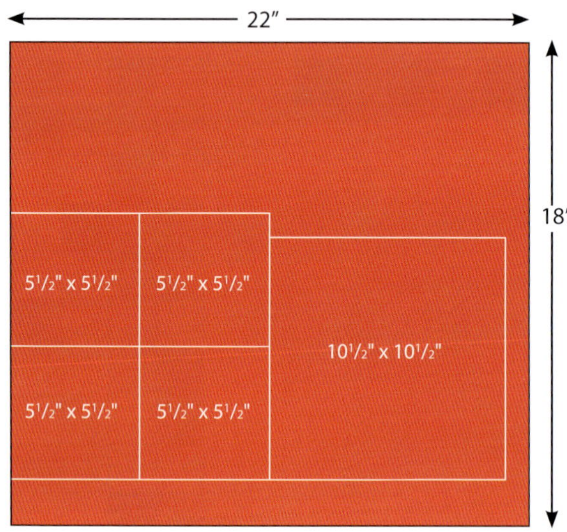

From fabric for backing:

- Cut 2 **backing** lengths 40" x 80½".

ASSEMBLING THE BLANKET

Read pages 8-15 before beginning your blanket. Use $^1/_4$" seam allowances throughout.

1. Sew 1 assorted dark **small square** and 1 assorted light **small square** together to make a **Unit 1**. Press the seam allowances toward the darker fabric. Make 2 Unit 1's.

2. Sew 2 Unit 1's together to make a **4-Patch Block**. Remove a few stitches in the previously sewn seam allowances to allow seam allowances in center to press in opposite directions like a pinwheel **(Fig.1)**.

3. Repeat Steps 1-2 to make a total of 20 4-Patch Blocks.

4. Sew 3 4-Patch Blocks and 2 **large squares** together to make **Row A**. Make 4 Row A's. Press seam allowances in one direction.

5. Sew 3 large squares and 2 4-Patch Blocks together to make **Row B**. Make 4 Row B's. Press seam allowances in the opposite direction.

6. Alternating direction of seam allowances, sew Rows together to make blanket top. Press seam allowances toward the bottom of the blanket top.

7. Matching long edges, sew **backing** lengths together; press seam allowances open. Trim backing to $50^1/_2$" x $80^1/_2$".

8. Refer to **Determining the Blanket Weight**, page 9, to determine the quantity of pellets needed for the blanket and how much to place in each pouch. This blanket has 160 pouches.

Unit 1 (make 2)

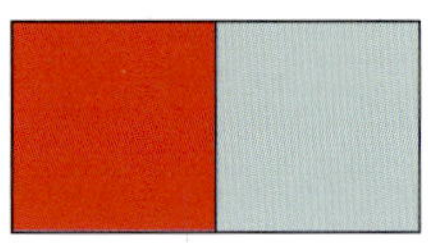

4-Patch Block

Fig. 1

Row A (make 4)

Row B (make 4)

Blanket Top

9. *Refer to **Assembling the Blanket**, pages 14-15, to assemble, fill, and close the blanket.* After sewing blanket top to backing, mark a line through the center of each large square (shown in red) both vertically and horizontally **(Fig. 2)**. Stitch vertically between each block, along each vertical seam of each Block, and across the large squares vertically where marked to make 10 vertical channels. Place determined amount of pellets in each channel. Stitch horizontally between each block, along each horizontal seam of each Block, and across the large squares horizontally where marked as you fill the channels to make 16 horizontal channels. Close the blanket.

Fig. 2

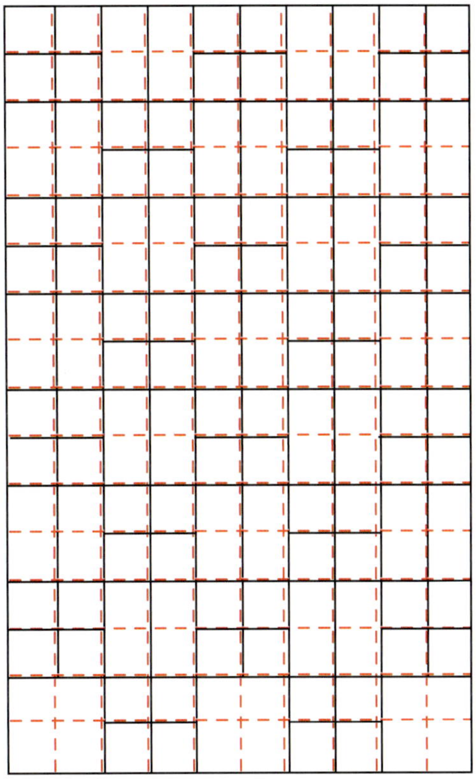

The following table provides the information necessary to make your blanket in other sizes.

	Youth Small	Youth Medium or Adult Small	Youth Large or Adult Medium	Adult Large
Finished Size	40" x 40"	40" x 50"	40" x 60"	50" x 70"
Fabric Requirements	8 assorted plaid flannel fat quarters $1^{3}/_{8}$ yds (1.3 m) of fabric for backing	10 assorted plaid flannel fat quarters $1^{5}/_{8}$ yds (1.5 m) of fabric for backing	12 assorted plaid flannel fat quarters $1^{7}/_{8}$ yds (1.7 m) of fabric for backing	18 assorted plaid flannel fat quarters $4^{1}/_{4}$ yds (3.9 m) of fabric for backing
Number of Blocks	16	20	24	35
Block Set	4 x 4	4 x 5	4 x 6	5 x 7
Pellet Pouches	64	80	96	140
Each Fat Quarter	**1 large square** $10^{1}/_{2}$" x $10^{1}/_{2}$" **4 small squares** $5^{1}/_{2}$" x $5^{1}/_{2}$"	**1 large square** $10^{1}/_{2}$" x $10^{1}/_{2}$" **4 small squares** $5^{1}/_{2}$" x $5^{1}/_{2}$"	**1 large square** $10^{1}/_{2}$" x $10^{1}/_{2}$" **4 small squares** $5^{1}/_{2}$" x $5^{1}/_{2}$"	**1 large square** $10^{1}/_{2}$" x $10^{1}/_{2}$" **4 small squares** $5^{1}/_{2}$" x $5^{1}/_{2}$"
Backing Cut Size	$40^{1}/_{2}$" x $40^{1}/_{2}$"	$40^{1}/_{2}$" x $50^{1}/_{2}$"	$40^{1}/_{2}$" x $60^{1}/_{2}$"	$50^{1}/_{2}$" x $70^{1}/_{2}$", pieced as necessary

plush lap *blanket*

Finished Size: 20" x 24"
(51 cm x 61 cm)

SHOPPING LIST

Yardage is based on 58"/60" (147 cm/152 cm) wide fabric with a usable width of 56" (142 cm).

- ☐ 1 yd (91 cm) of blue solid plush fabric

You will also need:

- ☐ 4 lbs (1814 grams) of plastic poly pellets
- ☐ walking foot
- ☐ size 14 (90) ballpoint sewing machine needle
- ☐ wrapping paper tube
- ☐ kitchen funnel
- ☐ measuring cup

CUTTING THE PIECES

*Follow **Rotary Cutting**, page 12, to cut fabric. All measurements include 1/2" seam allowances.*

From blue solid plush fabric:

- Cut two pieces 21" x 31" for **top** and **backing**.

ASSEMBLING THE LAP BLANKET TOP

Read pages 8-15 before beginning your blanket. Use 1/2" seam allowances throughout.

1. *Refer to **Assembling the Blanket**, pages 14-15, to assemble, fill and close the lap blanket.* After sewing lap blanket top to backing, stitch lengthwise approximately every 4" to make 5 long channels.
2. Place approximately 2 oz. of pellets in each channel. Let them fall all the way to the bottom. Stitch approximately every 4" as you fill the channels to make 6 channels. This will create 30 pouches. Close the lap blanket.

sherpa *blanket*

Adult Small, Finished Size: 40" x 60" (102 cm x 152 cm)

SHOPPING LIST

Yardage is based on 58"/60" (147 cm/152 cm) wide sherpa fabric with a usable width of 56" (142 cm) and 43"/44" (109 cm/112 cm) wide flannel fabric with a usable width of 40" (102 cm).

- ☐ 1$\frac{7}{8}$ yds (1.7 m) of sherpa fabric for blanket top
- ☐ 1$\frac{7}{8}$ yds (1.7 m) of plaid flannel fabric for blanket backing

You will also need:

- ☐ plastic poly pellets (see **Step 1**)
- ☐ walking foot
- ☐ size 14 (90) ballpoint sewing machine needle
- ☐ wrapping paper tube
- ☐ kitchen funnel
- ☐ measuring cup
- ☐ water-soluble fabric marking pen

CUTTING THE PIECES

*Follow **Rotary Cutting**, page 12, to cut fabric. All measurements include $\frac{1}{2}$" seam allowances.*

From sherpa fabric:

- Cut one piece 41" x 61" for **blanket top**.

From plaid flannel fabric:

- Cut one piece 41" x 61" for **backing**.

ASSEMBLING THE BLANKET

Read pages 8-15 before beginning your blanket. Use $\frac{1}{2}$" seam allowances throughout.

1. *Refer to **Determining the Blanket Weight**, page 9, to determine the quantity of pellets needed for the blanket and how much to place in each pouch. This blanket has 150 pouches.*

2. *Refer to **Assembling the Blanket**, pages 14-15, to assemble, fill, and close the lap blanket.* After sewing lap blanket top to backing, mark the vertical and horizontal stitching lines (shown in red) 4" apart on the blanket top (**Fig. 1**). Stitch vertically along each marked line to make 10 vertical channels. Place determined amount of pellets in each channel. Stitch horizontally along each marked line to make 15 horizontal channels. Close the blanket. If desired, topstitch $\frac{1}{2}$" from edge of blanket on all sides.

Fig. 1

rail *fence*

Adult Large, Finished Size: 42" x 72" (107 cm x 183 cm)
Finished Block Size: 6" x 6" (15 cm x 15 cm)

For information on other blanket sizes, refer to the table on page 36.

SHOPPING LIST

Yardage is based on 43"/44" (109 cm/112 cm) wide fabric with a usable width of 40" (102 cm). Jelly Rolls are 2$^1/_2$" (6.35 cm) wide x approximately 40" (102 cm).

- ☐ 2 Jelly Rolls or assorted 2$^1/_2$" (6.35 cm) wide strips totalling approximately 49 yds (45 m)
- ☐ 4$^3/_8$ yds (4 m) of fabric for backing
- ☐ plastic poly pellets (see **Step 5**, page 36)
- ☐ size 10 (70) sewing machine needle and size 14 (90) denim sewing machine needle
- ☐ walking foot
- ☐ wrapping paper tube
- ☐ kitchen funnel
- ☐ measuring cup

CUTTING THE PIECES

*Follow **Rotary Cutting**, page 12, to cut fabric. All measurements include $^1/_4$" seam allowances.*

From Jelly Roll strips:

- Cut 252 assorted **strips** 2$^1/_2$" x 7".

From fabric for backing:

- Cut 2 **backing** lengths 40" x 72$^1/_2$".

ASSEMBLING THE BLANKET

Read pages 8-15 before beginning your blanket. Use $^1/_4$" seam allowances throughout.

1. Matching long edges, sew 3 assorted **strips** together to make a **Block**. Press seam allowances to one side. Trim Block to 6$^1/_2$" x 6$^1/_2$". Make 84 Blocks.
2. Alternating direction of Blocks, sew 7 Blocks together to make a Row. Make 12 Rows. Press seam allowances in one direction.
3. Alternating direction of seam allowances, sew Rows together to make **Blanket Top**. Press seam allowances toward the bottom.

Block

Blanket Top

4. Matching right sides and long raw edges, sew backing lengths together. Press seam allowances open. Trim backing to $42\frac{1}{2}$" x $72\frac{1}{2}$".

5. Refer to **Determining the Blanket Weight**, page 9, to determine the quantity of pellets needed for the blanket and how much to place in each pouch. This blanket has 84 pouches.

6. *Refer to **Assembling the Blanket**, pages 14-15, to assemble, fill, and close the blanket.* Stitch vertically between each block (shown in red) to make 7 vertical channels **(Fig. 1)**. Place determined amount of pellets in each channel. Stitch horizontally between each Block as you fill the channels to make 12 horizontal channels. Close the blanket.

Fig. 1

The following table provides the information necessary to make your blanket in other sizes.

	Youth Small	Youth Medium or Adult Small	Youth Large or Adult Medium	Adult X-Large
Finished Size	36" x 48"	36" x 54"	36" x 60"	54" x 72"
Fabric Requirements	1 Jelly Roll or assorted $2\frac{1}{2}$" (6.35 cm) wide strips totalling approximately 28 yds (26 m) $1\frac{1}{2}$ yds (1.4 m) of fabric for backing	1 Jelly Roll or assorted $2\frac{1}{2}$" (6.35 cm) wide strips totalling approximately $31\frac{1}{2}$ yds (29 m) $1\frac{3}{4}$ yds (1.6 m) of fabric for backing	1 Jelly Roll or assorted $2\frac{1}{2}$" (6.35 cm) wide strips totalling approximately 35 yds (32 m) $1\frac{7}{8}$ yds (1.7 m) of fabric for backing	2 Jelly Rolls or assorted $2\frac{1}{2}$" (6.35 cm) wide strips totalling approximately 63 yds (58 m) $4\frac{3}{8}$ yds (4 m) of fabric for backing
Number of Blocks	48	54	60	108
Block Set	6 x 8	6 x 9	6 x 10	9 x 12
Pellet Pouches	48	54	60	108
Jelly Roll Strips	144 **strips** $2\frac{1}{2}$" x 7"	162 **strips** $2\frac{1}{2}$" x 7"	180 **strips** $2\frac{1}{2}$" x 7"	324 **strips** $2\frac{1}{2}$" x 7"
Backing Cut Size	$36\frac{1}{2}$" x $48\frac{1}{2}$"	$36\frac{1}{2}$" x $54\frac{1}{2}$"	$36\frac{1}{2}$" x $60\frac{1}{2}$"	$54\frac{1}{2}$" x $72\frac{1}{2}$", pieced as necessary

soccer *balls*

Youth Large/Adult Medium, Finished Size: 40" x 60" (102 cm x 152 cm)
Finished Block Size: 10" x 10" (25 cm x 25 cm)

For information on other blanket sizes, refer to the table on page 41.

SHOPPING LIST

Yardage is based on 43"/44" (109 cm/112 cm) wide fabric with a usable width of 40" (102 cm).

- ☐ $1^{1}/_{4}$ yds (1.1 m) of novelty print fabric for blocks
- ☐ $^{3}/_{4}$ yd (69 cm) of green solid fabric for blocks
- ☐ $^{3}/_{4}$ yd (69 cm) of blue solid fabric for blocks
- ☐ $1^{7}/_{8}$ yds (1.7 m) of fabric for backing
- ☐ plastic poly pellets (see **Step 5**, page 40)
- ☐ size 10 (70) sewing machine needle and size 14 (90) denim sewing machine needle
- ☐ walking foot
- ☐ wrapping paper tube
- ☐ kitchen funnel
- ☐ measuring cup
- ☐ water-soluble fabric marking pen

CUTTING THE PIECES

*Follow **Rotary Cutting**, page 12, to cut fabric. Cut all strips from the selvage-to-selvage width of the fabric. All measurements include $^{1}/_{4}$" seam allowances.*

From novelty print fabric:

- Cut 5 strips $7^{1}/_{2}$" wide. From these strips, cut 24 **center squares** $7^{1}/_{2}$" x $7^{1}/_{2}$".

From green solid fabric:

- Cut 4 strips 6" wide. From these strips, cut 24 squares 6" x 6". Cut each square once diagonally to make a total of 48 **triangles**.

From blue solid fabric:

- Cut 4 strips 6" wide. From these strips, cut 24 squares 6" x 6". Cut each square once diagonally to make a total of 48 **triangles**.

From backing fabric:

- Cut **backing** $40^{1}/_{2}$" x $60^{1}/_{2}$".

ASSEMBLING THE BLANKET

Read pages 8-15 before beginning your blanket. Use 1/4" seam allowances throughout.

1. Sew 2 blue **triangles** to opposite sides of 1 **center square**. Press seam allowances toward center square.

2. Sew 2 green **triangles** to remaining sides of 1 center square to make 1 **Block**. Press seam allowances toward center square. Trim each block to 10 1/2" x 10 1/2".

3. Sew 4 Blocks together to make a **Row**. Make 6 Rows. Press seam allowances in one direction.

4. Alternating direction of seam allowances, sew Rows together to make **Blanket Top**. Press seam allowances toward the bottom of the blanket top.

5. Refer to **Determining the Blanket Weight**, page 9, to determine the quantity of pellets needed for the blanket and how much to place in each pouch. This blanket has 96 pouches.

6. *Refer to* ***Assembling the Blanket****, pages 14-15, to assemble, fill, and close the blanket.* After sewing blanket top to backing, mark the vertical and horizontal stitching lines (shown in red) through the center of each Block on the blanket top **(Fig. 1)**. Stitch vertically between each Block and across the Blocks vertically where marked to make 8 vertical channels. Place determined amount of pellets in each channel. Stitch horizontally between each Block and across the Blocks horizontally where marked as you fill to make 12 horizontal channels. Close the blanket.

Block (make 24)

Blanket Top

Fig. 1

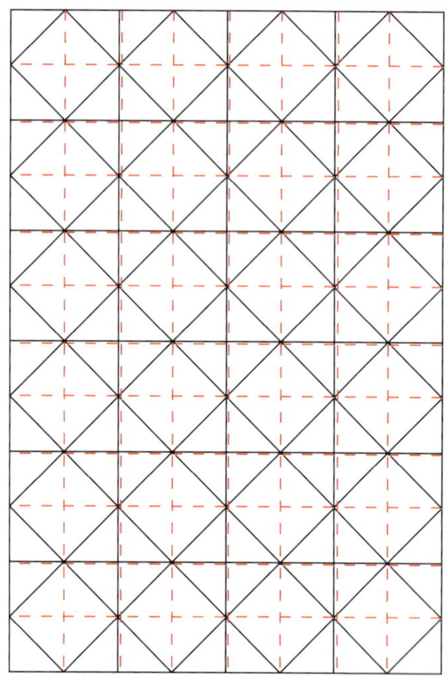

The following table provides the information necessary to make your blanket in other sizes.

	Youth Small	**Youth Medium or Adult Small**	**Adult Large**	**Adult X-Large**
Finished Size	40" x 40"	40" x 50"	40" x 70"	50" x 70"
Fabric Requirements	1 yd (91 cm) of novelty print fabric $^{5}/_{8}$ yd (57 cm) of green solid fabric $^{5}/_{8}$ yd (57 cm) of blue solid fabric $1^{1}/_{4}$ yds (1.1 m) of fabric for backing	1 yd (91 cm) of novelty print fabric $^{3}/_{4}$ yd (69 cm) of green solid fabric $^{3}/_{4}$ yd (69 cm) of blue solid fabric $1^{5}/_{8}$ yds (1.5 m) of fabric for backing	$1^{3}/_{8}$ yds (1.3 m) of novelty print fabric 1 yd (91 cm) of green solid fabric 1 yd (91 cm) of blue solid fabric $2^{1}/_{8}$ yds (1.9 m) of fabric for backing	$1^{5}/_{8}$ yds (1.5 m) of novelty print fabric $1^{1}/_{8}$ yds (1 m) of green solid fabric $1^{1}/_{8}$ yds (1 m) of blue solid fabric $4^{1}/_{4}$ yds (3.9 m) of fabric for backing
Number of Blocks	16	20	28	35
Block Set	4 x 4	4 x 5	4 x 7	5 x 7
Pellet Pouches	64	80	112	140
Novelty Print Fabric	16 **center squares** $7^{1}/_{2}$" x $7^{1}/_{2}$"	20 **center squares** $7^{1}/_{2}$" x $7^{1}/_{2}$"	28 **center squares** $7^{1}/_{2}$" x $7^{1}/_{2}$"	35 **center squares** $7^{1}/_{2}$" x $7^{1}/_{2}$"
Green Solid Fabric	Cut 16 squares 6" x 6". Cut once diagonally to make 32 **triangles.**	Cut 20 squares 6" x 6". Cut once diagonally to make 40 **triangles.**	Cut 28 squares 6" x 6". Cut once diagonally to make 56 **triangles.**	Cut 35 squares 6" x 6". Cut once diagonally to make 70 **triangles.**
Blue Solid Fabric	Cut 16 squares 6" x 6". Cut once diagonally to make 32 **triangles.**	Cut 20 squares 6" x 6". Cut once diagonally to make 40 **triangles.**	Cut 28 squares 6" x 6". Cut once diagonally to make 56 **triangles.**	Cut 35 squares 6" x 6". Cut once diagonally to make 70 **triangles.**
Backing Cut Size	$40^{1}/_{2}$" x $40^{1}/_{2}$"	$40^{1}/_{2}$" x $50^{1}/_{2}$"	$40^{1}/_{2}$" x $70^{1}/_{2}$"	$50^{1}/_{2}$" x $70^{1}/_{2}$", pieced as necessary

patriotic

Youth Large/Adult Medium, Finished Size: 40" x 60" (102 cm x 152 cm)
Finished Block Size: 10" x 10" (25 cm x 25 cm)

For information on other blanket sizes, refer to the table on page 47.

SHOPPING LIST

Yardage is based on 43"/44" (109 cm/112 cm) wide fabric with a usable width of 40" (102 cm).

- ☐ 1/4 yd (23 cm) of white solid fabric for blocks
- ☐ 1 yd (91 cm) of blue print fabric for blocks
- ☐ 1/2 yd (46 cm) of red print fabric for blocks
- ☐ 1 3/8 yds (1.3 m) of red/white/ blue print fabric for alternating blocks
- ☐ 1 7/8 yds (1.7 m) of fabric for backing
- ☐ plastic poly pellets (see **Step 9**, page 46)
- ☐ size 10 (70) sewing machine needle and size 14 (90) denim sewing machine needle
- ☐ walking foot
- ☐ wrapping paper tube
- ☐ kitchen funnel
- ☐ measuring cup
- ☐ water-soluble fabric marking pen

CUTTING THE PIECES

*Follow **Rotary Cutting**, page 12, to cut fabric. Cut all strips from the selvage-to-selvage width of the fabric. All measurements include 1/4" seam allowances.*

From white solid fabric:

- Cut 2 strips 3 7/8" wide. From these strips, cut 12 **small squares** 3 7/8" x 3 7/8".

From blue print fabric:

- Cut 5 strips 3 7/8" wide. From these strips, cut 48 **small squares** 3 7/8" x 3 7/8".
- Cut 3 strips 4 3/8" wide. From these strips, cut 24 **medium squares** 4 3/8" x 4 3/8".

From red print fabric:

- Cut 3 strips 4 3/8" wide. From these strips, cut 24 **medium squares** 4 3/8" x 4 3/8".

From red/white/blue print fabric:

- Cut 4 strips 10 1/2" wide. From these strips, cut 12 **large squares** 10 1/2" x 10 1/2".

From fabric for backing:

- Cut **backing** 40 1/2" x 60 1/2".

ASSEMBLING THE BLANKET

Read pages 8-15 before beginning your blanket. Use 1/4" seam allowances throughout.

1. Draw a diagonal line on wrong side of each red print **medium square**. With right sides together, place 1 red print medium square on top of 1 blue print **medium square**. Stitch seam 1/4" from each side of drawn line **(Fig. 1)**.

2. Cut along drawn line and press seam allowances toward darker fabric to make 2 **Triangle-Squares**. Make a total of 48 Triangle-Squares. Trim each Triangle-Square to $3\frac{7}{8}$" x $3\frac{7}{8}$".

3. Sew 2 blue print **small squares** and 1 Triangle-Square together to make **Unit 1**. Make 24 Unit 1's.

4. Sew 2 Triangle-Squares and 1 white solid **small square** together to make **Unit 2**. Make 12 Unit 2's.

5. Sew 2 Unit 1's and 1 Unit 2 together to make a **Block**. Make 12 Blocks.

6. Sew 2 **large squares** and 2 Blocks together to make **Row 1**. Make 3 Row 1's. Press seam allowances in one direction.

7. Sew 2 Blocks and 2 **large squares** together to make **Row 2**. Make 3 Row 2's. Press seam allowances in the opposite direction.

Fig. 1

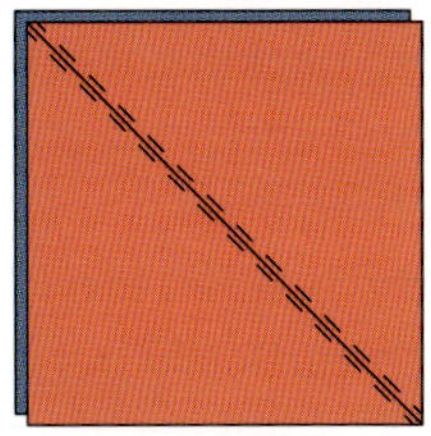

Triangle-Square (make 48)

Unit 1 (make 24)

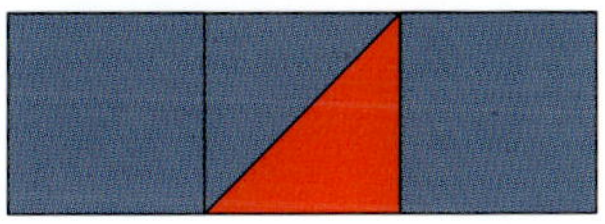

Unit 2 (make 12)

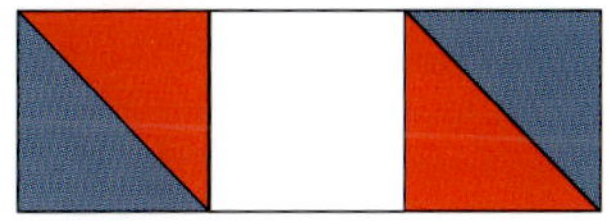

Block (make 12)

Row 1 (make 3)

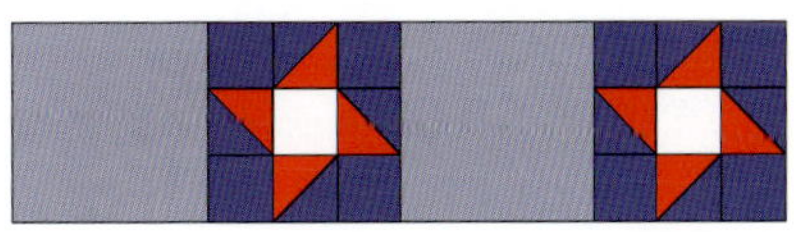

Row 2 (make 3)

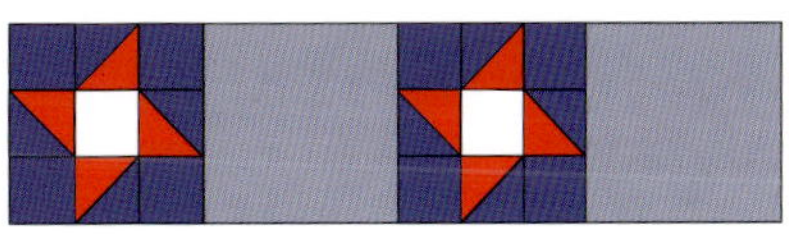

8. Alternating Rows and direction of seam allowances, sew Row 1's and 2's together to make **Blanket Top**. Press seam allowances toward the bottom of the blanket top.

9. Refer to **Determining the Blanket Weight**, page 9, to determine the quantity of pellets needed for the blanket and how much to place in each pouch. This blanket has 216 pouches.

10. *Refer to **Assembling the Blanket**, pages 14-15, to assemble, fill, and close the blanket.* After sewing blanket top to backing, mark the vertical and horizontal stitching lines (shown in red) on the blanket top **(Fig. 2)**. Stitch vertically between each block, along each vertical seam of each Block, and across the large squares vertically where marked to make 12 vertical channels. Place determined amount of pellets in each channel. Stitch in the ditch horizontally between each block, along each horizontal seam of each block, and across the large squares horizontally where marked as you fill the channels to make 18 horizontal channels. Close the blanket.

Blanket Top

Fig. 2

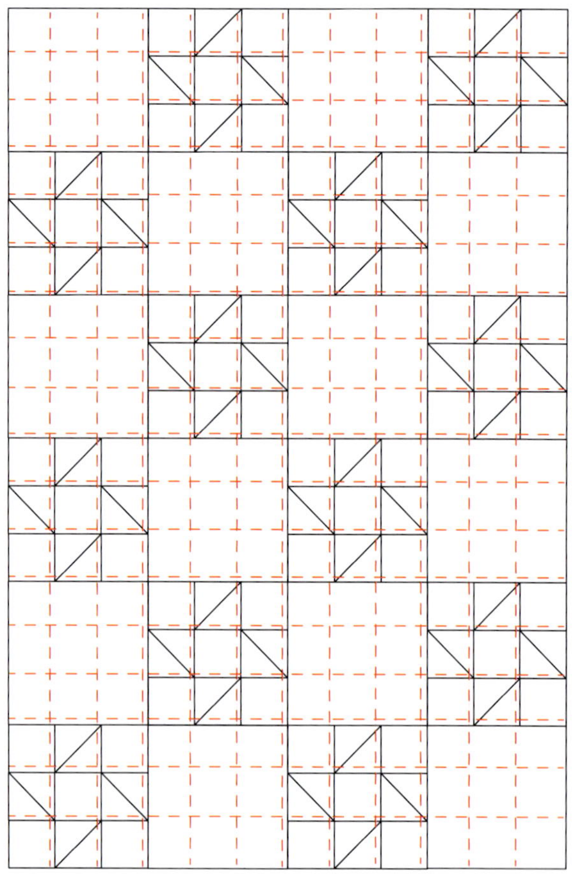

The following table provides the information necessary to make your blanket in other sizes.

	Youth Small	Youth Medium or Adult Small	Adult Large	Adult X-Large
Finished Size	40" x 40"	40" x 50"	40" x 80"	50" x 80"
Fabric Requirements	1/8 yd (11 cm) of white solid fabric 3/4 yd (69 cm) of blue print fabric 3/8 yd (34 cm) of red print fabric 1 yd (91 cm) of red/white/blue print fabric 1 1/4 yds (1.1 m) of fabric for backing	1/8 yd (11 cm) of white solid fabric 7/8 yd (80 cm) of blue print fabric 1/2 yd (46 cm) of red print fabric 1 3/8 yds (1.3 m) of red/white/blue print fabric 1 5/8 yds (1.5 m) of fabric for backing	1/4 yd (23 cm) of white solid fabric 1 3/8 yds (1.1 m) of blue print fabric 5/8 yd (57 cm) of red print fabric 2 yds (1.8 m) of red/white/blue print fabric 2 3/8 yds (2.2 m) of fabric for backing	1/4 yd (23 cm) of white solid fabric 1 5/8 yds (1.4 m) of blue print fabric 3/4 yd (69 cm) of red print fabric 2 1/4 yds (2.1 m) of red/white/blue print fabric 4 3/4 yds (4.3 m) of fabric for backing
Number of Blocks	16	20	32	40
Block Set	4 x 4	4 x 5	4 x 8	5 x 8
Pellet Pouches	144	180	288	360
White Solid Fabric	8 **small squares** 3 7/8" x 3 7/8"	10 **small squares** 3 7/8" x 3 7/8"	16 **small squares** 3 7/8" x 3 7/8"	20 **small squares** 3 7/8" x 3 7/8"
Blue Print Fabric	32 **small squares** 3 7/8" x 3 7/8" 16 **medium squares** 4 3/8" x 4 3/8"	40 **small squares** 3 7/8" x 3 7/8" 20 **medium squares** 4 3/8" x 4 3/8"	64 **small squares** 3 7/8" x 3 7/8" 32 **medium squares** 4 3/8" x 4 3/8"	80 **small squares** 3 7/8" x 3 7/8" 40 **medium squares** 4 3/8" x 4 3/8"
Red Print Fabric	16 **medium squares** 4 3/8" x 4 3/8"	20 **medium squares** 4 3/8" x 4 3/8"	32 **medium squares** 4 3/8" x 4 3/8"	40 **medium squares** 4 3/8" x 4 3/8"
Red/White/Blue Print Fabric	8 **large squares** 10 1/2" x 10 1/2"	10 **large squares** 10 1/2" x 10 1/2"	16 **large squares** 10 1/2" x 10 1/2"	20 **large squares** 10 1/2" x 10 1/2"
Fabric for Backing	40 1/2" x 40 1/2"	40 1/2" x 50 1/2"	40 1/2" x 80 1/2"	50 1/2" x 80 1/2", pieced as necessary

weighted cuddle blanket

Finished Size: 52" x $74^1/_2$" (132 cm x 189 cm)

SHOPPING LIST

Yardage is based on 58"/60" (147 cm/152 cm) plush fleece fabric with a usable width of 56" (142 cm).

- ☐ $3^1/_2$ yds (3.2 m) of solid-color plush fleece fabric for cuddle blanket body, sleeves, and backing
- ☐ $^1/_2$ yd (46 cm) of plaid plush fleece fabric for neck and sleeve trim

You will also need:

- ☐ 8 cups of plastic poly pellets
- ☐ walking foot
- ☐ size 14 (90) ballpoint sewing machine needle
- ☐ wrapping paper tube
- ☐ kitchen funnel
- ☐ measuring cup
- ☐ disappearing ink fabric marking pen
- ☐ tracing paper

CUTTING THE PIECES

*Follow **Rotary Cutting**, page 12, to cut fabric. All measurements include $^1/_2$" seam allowances.*

From solid-color plush fleece fabric:

- Cut cuddle blanket **body** 56" x $72^1/_2$".
- Cut 2 **sleeves** 23" x 20".
- Cut **backing** 20" x 24".

From plaid plush fleece fabric:

- Cut **neck trim** 7" x 56".
- Cut 2 **sleeve trim** $8^1/_2$" x 23".

From tracing paper:

- Trace sleeve opening pattern, page 62; cut out.

ASSEMBLING THE BLANKET

Use $^1/_2$" seam allowances throughout.

1. Matching right sides, sew neck trim to one short edge of cuddle blanket body.
2. Fold remaining long edge of neck trim 1" to wrong side then 1" to wrong side again; stitch in place.
3. Fold opposite edge (bottom) of cuddle blanket body 1" to wrong side then 1" to wrong side again; stitch in place.
4. Fold each side edge of cuddle blanket body 1" to wrong side then 1" to wrong side again; stitch in place.

5. Refer to **Fig. 1** to pin paper circle on cuddle blanket; cut out sleeve opening. Stitch $^{3}/_{8}$" from raw edge around sleeve opening.

6. Using scissors, cut small notches outside the stitching line, dividing the sleeve opening into fourths (top, bottom, and sides).

7. Repeat Steps 5-6 for remaining sleeve opening on adjacent corner of blanket.

8. Fold one long edge of one sleeve trim 1" to wrong side then 1" to wrong side again; stitch in place.

9. Matching long raw edges, sew sleeve trim to one sleeve.

10. To make sleeve, match right sides and sew long edges together.

11. With the seam at the bottom, lay sleeve flat. Cut small notches, dividing the raw edge of the sleeve into fourths.

12. Matching right sides and notches, pin and sew the sleeve in the opening.

13. Repeat Steps 8-12 to make and insert remaining sleeve.

14. Mark the vertical and horizontal stitching lines (shown in red) 4" apart on right side of the backing **(Fig. 2)**.

15. Place backing on wrong side of body **(Fig. 3)**. Stitch in place along sides and bottom, close to edges.

16. Stitch along each marked vertical line. Place about 4 oz. of pellets in each channel. Stitch horizontally along the marked line to make a horizontal row of pouches. Continue filling and sewing horizontal rows of pouches in this manner. Stitch across the top of the backing to close top row of pouches.

Fig. 1

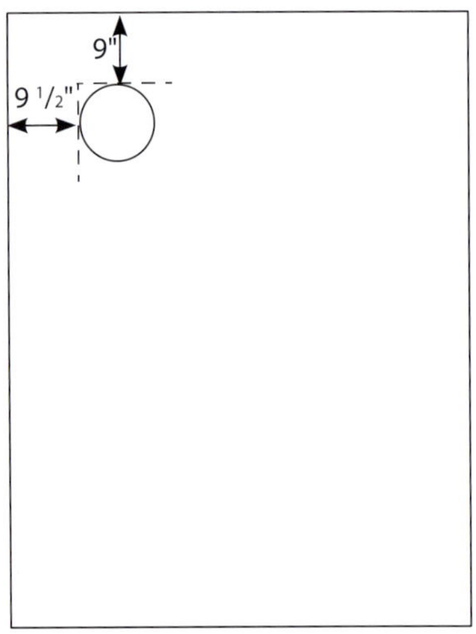

Fig. 2

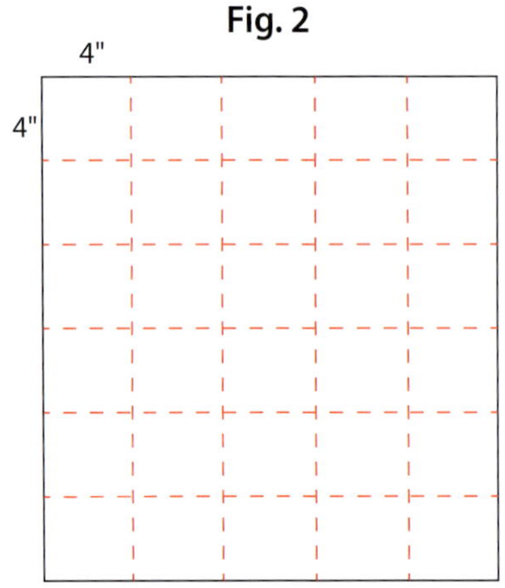

Fig. 3

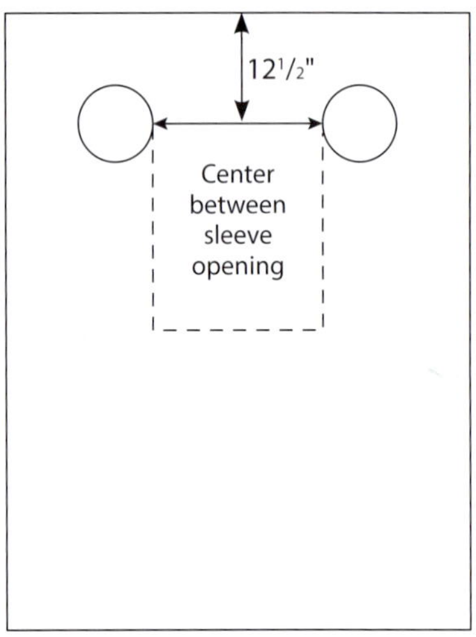

weighted *eye mask*

SHOPPING LIST

Yardage is based on 58"/60" (147 cm/152 cm) wide plush fleece fabric with a usable width of 56" (142 cm).

- ☐ 1/4 yd (23 cm) of plush fleece

You will also need:

- ☐ 13" (33 cm) of 3/4" (19 mm) wide elastic
- ☐ 1 cup plastic poly pellets
- ☐ walking foot
- ☐ size 14 (90) ballpoint sewing machine needle
- ☐ kitchen funnel
- ☐ measuring cup
- ☐ water-soluble fabric marking pen
- ☐ tape measure
- ☐ large safety pin

CUTTING THE PIECES

All measurements include 1/2" seam allowances.

From plush fleece:

- Using pattern, page 63, cut 2 eye masks.
- Cut 1 band 3" x 16".

ASSEMBLING THE EYE MASK

Use 1/2" seam allowances.

1. Using scissors, make small snips in one eye mask where indicated on pattern to mark placement for band.

2. Matching right sides and long raw edges, fold band in half. Sew along long edge, leaving ends open. Turn band right side out.

3. Measure around back of head from temple to temple. Cut elastic to this length.

4. Attach safety pin to one end of elastic. Insert safety pin in one end of band. Use safety pin to push elastic through band, pinning ends of elastic even with band ends. Baste elastic to band ends.

5. Baste band ends to 1 eye mask at snips.

6. Matching right sides, sew eye masks together with band sandwiched between layers and leaving an opening for turning along the straight edge Be careful not to catch band in stitching. Turn mask right side out.

7. Using funnel and measuring cup, place pellets inside eye mask. Sew opening closed.

huggable *neck wrap*

Finished Size: 8" x 36" (20 cm x 91 cm)

SHOPPING LIST

Yardage is based on 58"/60" (147 cm/152 cm) wide fabric with a usable width of 56" (142 cm).

- ☐ 5/8 yd (57 cm) of gray solid plush fabric

You will also need:

- ☐ 3 lbs (1361 grams) of plastic poly pellets
- ☐ walking foot
- ☐ size 14 (90) ballpoint sewing machine needle
- ☐ wrapping paper tube
- ☐ kitchen funnel
- ☐ measuring cup

CUTTING THE PIECES

*Follow **Rotary Cutting**, page 12, to cut fabric. All measurements include 1/2" seam allowances.*

From gray solid plush fabric:

- Cut two pieces 9" x 37" for **top** and **backing**.

ASSEMBLING THE NECK WRAP

Read pages 8-15 before beginning your wrap. Use 1/2" seam allowances throughout.

1. *Refer to **Assembling the Blanket**, pages 14-15, to assemble, fill and close the neck wrap.* After sewing neck wrap top to backing, stitch lengthwise through the center to make 2 long channels.
2. Place approximately 2 1/2 oz. of pellets in each channel. Let them fall all the way to the bottom. Stitch every 4" as you fill the channels to make 9 channels. This will create 18 pouches. Close the neck wrap.

pinwheel *lap blanket*

Finished Size: 18" x 30" (46 cm x 76 cm)
Finished Block Size: 10" x 10" (25 cm x 25 cm)

SHOPPING LIST

Yardage is based on 43"/44" (109 cm/112 cm) wide fabric with a usable width of 40" (102 cm).

- ☐ 1/4 yd (23 cm) of yellow print fabric
- ☐ 1/4 yd (23 cm) of green print fabric
- ☐ 1/4 yd (23 cm) of blue print fabric
- ☐ 1/2 yd (46 cm) of black solid fabric
- ☐ 5/8 yd (57 cm) of black flannel fabric for backing
- ☐ 4 lbs (1814 grams) of plastic poly pellets
- ☐ walking foot
- ☐ size 10 (70) sewing machine needle and size 14 (90) denim sewing machine needle
- ☐ wrapping paper tube
- ☐ kitchen funnel
- ☐ measuring cup

CUTTING THE PIECES

*Follow **Rotary Cutting**, page 12, to cut fabric. Cut all strips from the selvage-to-selvage width of the fabric. All measurements include 1/4" seam allowances.*

From yellow print fabric:

- Cut 1 strip 6" wide. From this strip, cut 2 **squares** 6" x 6".

From green print fabric:

- Cut 1 strip 6" wide. From this strip, cut 2 **squares** 6" x 6".

From blue print fabric:

- Cut 1 strip 6" wide. From this strip, cut 2 **squares** 6" x 6".

From black solid fabric:

- Cut 1 strip 6" wide. From this strip, cut 6 **squares** 6" x 6".
- Cut 2 **borders** 4 1/2" x 30 1/2".

From black flannel fabric:

- Cut **backing** 18 1/2" x 30 1/2".

ASSEMBLING THE LAP BLANKET

Read pages 8-15 before beginning your blanket. Use 1/4" seam allowances throughout.

1. Draw a diagonal line on wrong side of each bright-colored **square**. With right sides together, place 1 bright-colored square on top of 1 black square. Stitch seam 1/4" from each side of drawn line **(Fig. 1)**.

2. Cut along drawn line and press seam allowances toward darker fabric to make 2 **Triangle-Squares**. Make a total of 12 Triangle-Squares (4 of each color). Trim each Triangle-Square to 5 1/2" x 5 1/2".

3. Sew 4 matching Triangle-Squares together to make a Pinwheel Block. Make 3 Pinwheel Blocks.

4. Sew Pinwheel Blocks together. Press seam allowances in one direction.

5. Sew 1 border to each long edge to make **Lap Blanket Top**. Top should measure 18 1/2" x 30 1/2".

6. *Refer to **Assembling the Blanket**, pages 14-15, to assemble, fill, and close the lap blanket.* After sewing lap blanket top to backing, stitch along each seam between the border and the Pinwheel Blocks and through the center of the Pinwheel Blocks to make 4 long channels. Aligning the line with each seam in each pieced Block, mark stitching lines across each border.

7. Aligning the line with each seam between each Triangle-Square, mark stitching lines across each border.

8. Place 1/2 cup of pellets in each channel. Let them fall all the way to the bottom. Stitch along the marked lines as you fill the channels to make 6 channels. This will create 24 pouches. Close the lap blanket.

Fig. 1

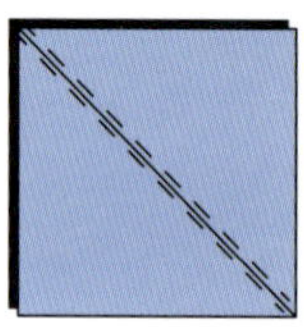

Triangle-Square (make 12)

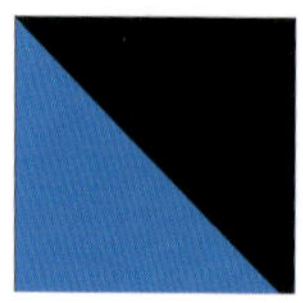

Pinwheel Block (make 3)

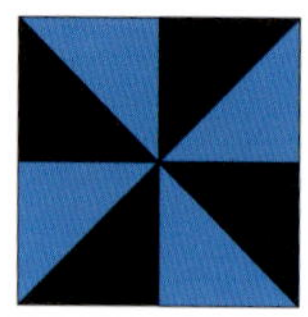

Lap Blanket Top

pinwheel *neck wrap*

Finished Size: 8" x 36" (20 cm x 91 cm)
Finished Block Size: 3" x 3" (8 cm x 8 cm)

SHOPPING LIST

Yardage is based on 43"/44" (109 cm/112 cm) wide fabric with a usable width of 40" (102 cm).

- ☐ 1/4 yd (23 cm) of yellow print fabric
- ☐ 1/4 yd (23 cm) of green print fabric
- ☐ 1/4 yd (23 cm) of blue print fabric
- ☐ 1/4 yd (23 cm) of purple print fabric
- ☐ 3/8 yd (34 cm) of black solid fabric
- ☐ 3/8 yd (34 cm) of black flannel fabric for backing
- ☐ 3 lbs (1361 grams) of plastic poly pellets
- ☐ size 10 (70) sewing machine needle and size 14 (90) denim sewing machine needle
- ☐ walking foot
- ☐ wrapping paper tube
- ☐ kitchen funnel
- ☐ measuring cup

CUTTING THE PIECES

*Follow **Rotary Cutting**, page 12, to cut fabric. Cut all strips from the selvage-to-selvage width of the fabric. All measurements include 1/4" seam allowances.*

From yellow print fabric:
- Cut 1 strip 4" wide. From this strip, cut 3 **squares** 4" x 4".

From green print fabric:
- Cut 1 strip 4" wide. From this strip, cut 3 **squares** 4" x 4".

From blue print fabric:
- Cut 1 strip 4" wide. From this strip, cut 3 **squares** 4" x 4".

From purple print fabric:
- Cut 1 strip 4" wide. From this strip, cut 3 **squares** 4" x 4".

From black solid fabric:
- Cut 2 strips 4" wide. From these strips, cut 12 **squares** 4" x 4".
- Cut 2 **borders** 1 1/2" x 36 1/2".

From black flannel fabric:
- Cut **backing** 8 1/2" x 36 1/2".

ASSEMBLING THE NECK WRAP

Read pages 8-15 before beginning your blanket. Use 1/4" seam allowances throughout.

1. Draw a diagonal line on wrong side of each bright-colored **square**. With right sides together, place 1 bright-colored square on top of 1 black square. Stitch seam 1/4" from each side of drawn line **(Fig. 1)**.

2. Cut along drawn line and press seam allowances toward darker fabric to make 2 **Triangle-Squares**. Make a total of 24 Triangle-Squares (6 of each color). Trim each Triangle-Square to 3 1/2" x 3 1/2".

3. Sew 2 matching Triangle-Squares together to make a Flying Geese. Repeat with all triangles to make a total of 12 Flying Geese (3 of each color).

4. Sew Flying Geese together along long edges to make neck wrap center. Press seam allowances in one direction.

5. Sew 1 border to each long edge to make **Neck Wrap Top**. Top should measure 8 1/2" x 36 1/2".

6. *Refer to **Assembling the Blanket**, pages 14-15, to assemble, fill, and close the neck wrap.* After sewing neck wrap top to backing, stitch through the center of the Flying Geese to make 2 long channels. Aligning the line with each seam between each Flying Geese, mark stitching lines across each border.

7. Place approximately 2 oz. of pellets in each vertical channel. Let them fall all the way to the bottom. Stitch in the ditch between each Flying Geese and across marked borders as you fill the channels to make 12 channels. This will create 24 pouches. Close the blanket.

Fig. 1

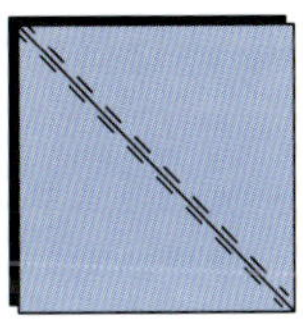

Triangle-Square (make 24)

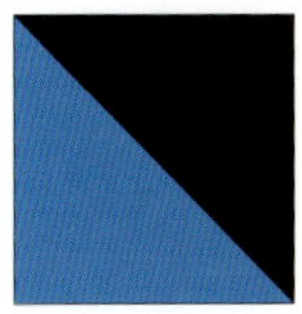

Neck Wrap Top

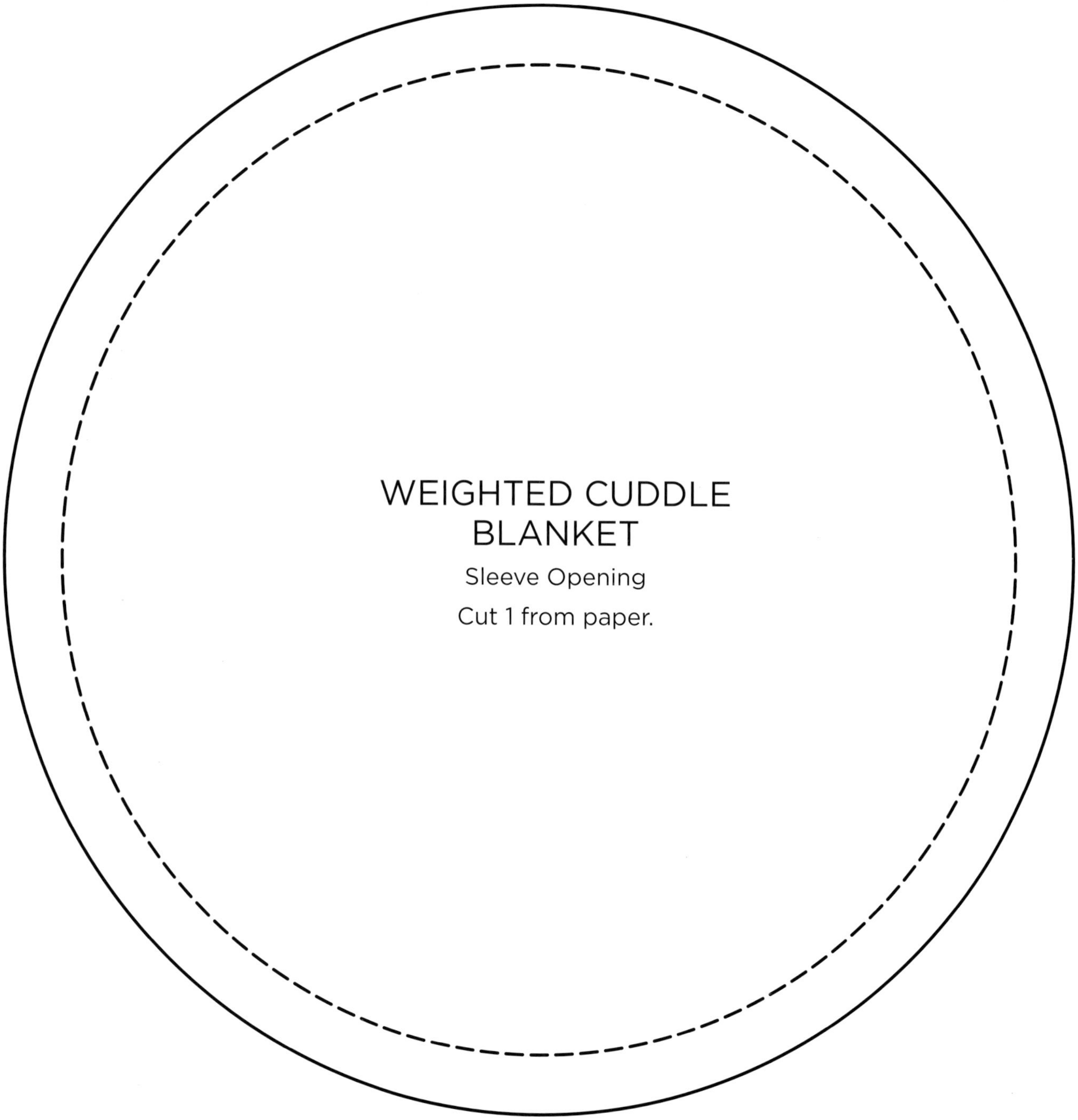
WEIGHTED CUDDLE BLANKET
Sleeve Opening
Cut 1 from paper.

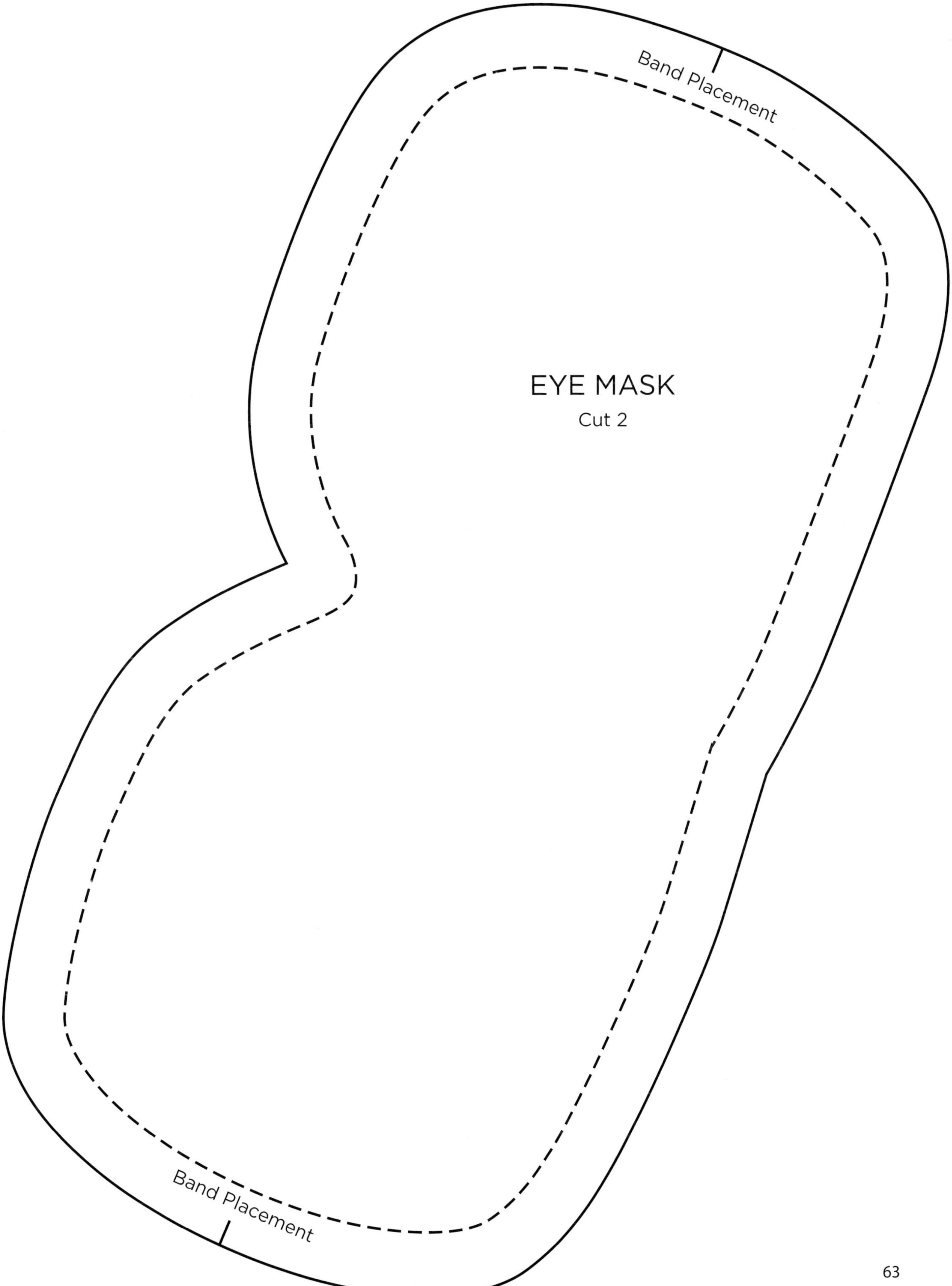
Band Placement
EYE MASK
Cut 2
Band Placement

We would like to thank Fabric Editions, Inc. for supplying some of the fabrics used in our blankets.

We would also like to thank Nelwyn Gray, Delorse Richards, and Billie Steward for sewing some of our blankets.

Production Team: Designer – Kelly Reider and Billie Steward; Technical Editor – Lisa Lancaster; Editorial Writer – Susan Frantz Wiles and Paige Yutsus; Senior Graphic Artist - Lora Puls; Associate Graphic Artist - Kytanna McFarlin; Photographer - Jason Masters; Photography Stylists – Stephanie Moore and Lori Wenger.

Made in China